HOW TO GET AN
AUTISTIC CHILD
TO KISS YOU

A Physiotherapist share her personal experience of how she treated a 3 years old boy who used to live in his own world in the past 3 years In 5 days time Milly successfully treated him to emotionally embrace his mom and kiss her on the lips for the first time in his life

Milly Ng MCSP(UK) RP(HK) RP(Australia)

WORKBOOK PRESS LLC
187 E Warm Springs Rd,
Suite B285, Las Vegas, NV 89119, USA

Website:	https://workbookpress.com/
Hotline:	1-888-818-4856
Email:	admin@workbookpress.com

Ordering Information:
Quantity sales. Special discounts are available on quantity purchases by corporations, associations, and others.
For details, contact the publisher at the address above.

Library of Congress Control Number:
ISBN-13:   978-1-958176-06-1 (Paperback Version)
             978-1-958176-07-8 (Digital Version)

REV. DATE: 08/04/2022

HOW TO GET AN
AUTISTIC CHILD
TO KISS YOU

A Physiotherapist share her personal experience of how she treated
a 3 years old boy who lived in his own world in the past 3 years.
In 5 days' time, Milly successfully treated him to emotionally
embraced his mom, and kissed her on the lips
for the first time in his life.

HOW TO GET AN AUTISTIC CHILD TO KISS YOU

Milly NG

MCSP (UK) RP (Australia) RP (HK)

CONTENTS

Introduction   2

My girlfriend's nephew – Adam   4

Seek treatment   6

Tongue Acupuncture   9

How I Made Adam Kissed His Mom 11

Change the Life   14

Acknowledgement   16

Milly attended Autism Awareness Day in Western Australia

Introduction

Of course, I don't mean to hold the child up and force him to kiss
you on the lips. What I mean is to get the child to kiss you out of his own free will without any coercion.

Then you might argue, if he wants to kiss you from the bottom of his heart, then he is not considered autistic anymore.

Yes, you are right, that's exactly what I meant!

This is my personal experience I am going to relate to you. I made a very autistic kid to kiss his mom in 5 days' time and in fact, I also made him not to follow his mom's idea of "Go kiss Auntie Milly!" and saved me from the wet kiss. You know I am a very modest person; I am not used to this western culture of being kissed by a stranger.

Before I continue my story, there are other suggestions on how you can make an autistic kid to kiss you.

Maybe you can hypnotize the child to get him follow what you want him to do. But this is not a big diff erence than physically hold him up to kiss you. You are just manipulating him mentally.

But the point is, to get the child look into your eyes in order to hypnotize him is diffi cult. How would you be able to communicate with him and get him to follow you is a problem.

Back to square one, one need to treat an autistic kid to come out of his Autism is the final solution. It so happened that it took me 5 days to realize it, which in fact should be much sooner, maybe 3 days. Will tell you why I am so confi dent!

Most autistic kids tend to live in their own world, do their own things, read their own books, play their own games, most of the time repeatedly. They do not have eye contacts with another human being, including their parents and siblings. They refused to talk, refused to communicate, some of them even refused to chew food. It is indeed a headache having an autistic kid in the family.

My girlfriend's nephew - Adam

Tina, my girlfriend of 10 years, one day asked me if I treat Autistic kid. Her nephew, will turn 3 years old in a few months, was diagnosed with Autism. He seldom talked and seem to be indifferent to his surroundings. At first, they suspected if he has a hearing problem. But the hearing test was normal. And he would feel startled by loud noises. Also, he would not eat solid food and refused to chew.

Harry, Adam's father was like that when he was at Adam's age as recalled by grandma. So Harry just kept preparing the food grinding to a paste for the son and hope that Adam will grow out of his condition when he becomes older.

They felt very upset and embarrassed when going out for family gatherings meeting other relatives as Adam would not socialize with other kids. Some relatives even asked if he is deaf as he doesn't talk nor respond to the surroundings. So they would try to avoid any social gatherings which make them even more isolated.

The problem intensified when Adam approached 3 years old as he needed to enroll into kindergarten but no school wanted to take him as he refused to neither talk nor communicate at the interview.

Finally, with the referral of some friends and some donations to the school, they managed to get a place in a preschool for Adam. But then life is still not easy as few days before Christmas, the head teacher informed Ada, Adam's mom not to take Adam to the school

Christmas party because they do not want Adam to interfere with the other kids in the party.

Ada was so upset hearing that. It is even worse than asking her not to attend the company's party. She went home and cried the whole night with husband Harry.

It has come to a tipping point they decided they have to do something about it. They cannot wait for the problem to grow out on its own anymore.

Seek Treatment

So they asked around, Google for resources. It came up with very limited support at that time in 2012. Tina asked me if I can help. I told her to bring Adam to me as I had experience treating autistic kids and other pediatric cases with good results.

In 2012, I was still running my busy Private Physiotherapy Clinic in Hong Kong. In a private clinic, you would be able to encounter a lot of different cases every day in the highly densely populated six and a half million people of Hong Kong. I was very lucky to set up my clinic in the most prestigious medical building - The famous 'Central Building'. People just thought that any doctor or therapist who managed to run a clinic there must be highly qualifi ed, either a respectable professor from the University or a teaching consultant from a well-known organization. So for a Physiotherapist who set up her office there for 20 years must be really something. For that reason, I see a lot of diffi cult cases that can't find a cure elsewhere would knock on my door to check if I can offer any solution. So incidentally, I was famous treating a lot of cases that conventional medicine would think there was no cure. * So before Adam, I have treated quite a few cases of Autistic kids though not as severe as the condition of Adam.

As you might now gathered that I am quite an experienced Physiotherapist who set up my private clinic for 20 years and not a conventional one who helped to mobilize the arms and legs or put on a TENS machine over some painful spot to alleviate the pain or hold your hand to guide you to walk those type of Physiotherapist.

I like to take up difficult cases and found it the more difficult, the more challenging. Example, I once turned a badly crushed hand (so bad that 2 fingers detached) back to 100% normal to work again as a decorator in one and a half months. I also turned a 6 years old blind boy with brain damage few months old leaving him with 10% vision to become normal again in 2 months' time.

So hearing Tina's nephew's condition, I was in fact very eager to treat. As I am passionate to be able to change people's life. But somehow Ada would prefer to try something else instead of bringing Adam to me. I think it is because I am Tina's friend.

The Difficult Cases I Encountered in my 20 Years of Private Practice

I have successfully treated 2 cases of Rare Adolescent Urinary incontinence that all methods failed over the years - the 18 years old boy took 10 sessions while the 13 years old boy took 30 sessions, 100% cured.

Accidental findings that my treatment can lift the sagging breast of a lady patient after her work injury in the airplane by a flying food trolley against one of her breasts, the treated breast lifted up significantly compared to the non-treated side. (Lift Sagging breast. Image E on page 19)

I can easily correct scoliosis in 12 minutes. (Correct Scoliosis in 12 min. Image H on page 20)

I saved a raw wound from skin graft by healing it in 15 Days. (Raw wound saving patient from Skin graft. Image I on page 20)

I can grow hair for patients who has been bald for more than 15 years in as little as 9 days. (Grow hair. Image D on page 19)

*I have treated a case of Spinal Cord injury at C4 level to be able to sit up, stand and walk with aids in one month saved her from becoming a quadriplegic and wheelchair bound for life.

Tongue Acupuncture

They brought Adam to try acupuncture on the tongue.

Please don't get me wrong. I do not have any intention to say anything inappropriate about other methods of treatment. To me, any treatment that can bring about result is good. But I don't really know how they manage to get a 3 years old boy to cooperate with them to complete the procedure.

The boy opens his mouth to stick out his tongue, and I poke a few acupuncture needles on the sensitive tongue and leave it there.

Incredible!

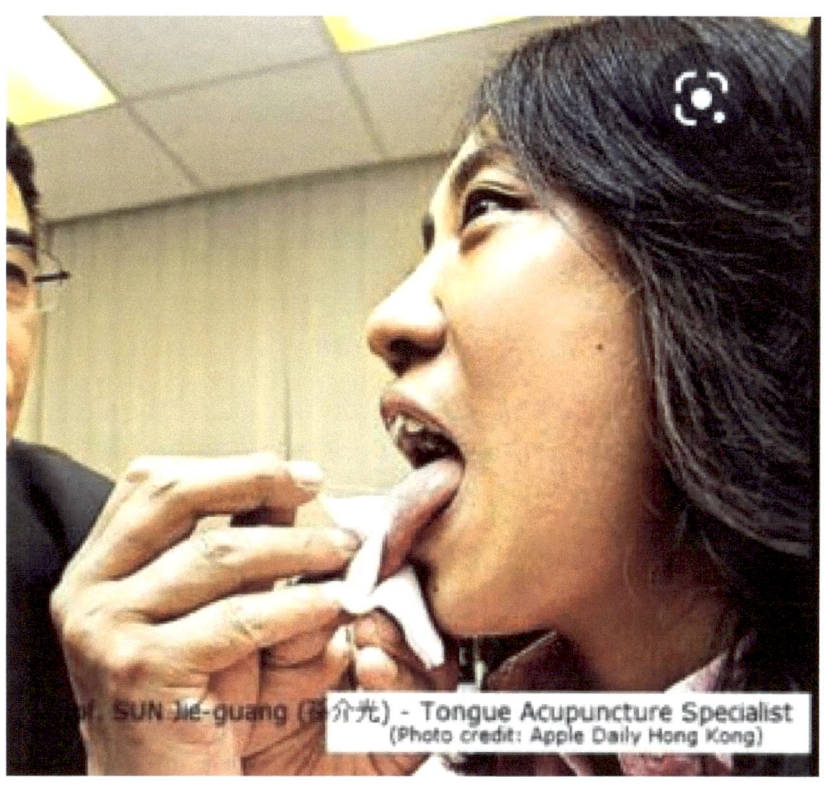

Example of Tongue Acupuncture

How I made Adam Kissed His Mom on the Lips

So after a few weeks, finally, Harry carried the three and a half

years old Adam to my clinic. You can imagine how frightened Adam would be being carried to another clinic, not knowing what will happen this time. Would they poke some more needles elsewhere?

The only way he can protest is screaming at the height of his voice and struggled to go away.

I explained to Harry what I will do and asked him to put Adam face up on the treatment table. But as Harry worried Adam would run away, as he might have experienced with the tongue acupuncture, so Harry very efficiently climbed up to sit on top of Adam to fi x him on the bed and let me work on his forehead.

It is, in fact, a very soothing procedure with no pain at all. I just gently stroke the forehead with the two probe electrodes directing the Microcurrent to the frontal part of the brain. But no matter what I do, Adam would just keep his eyes tightly shut and kept on screaming at the height of his voice throughout the 20 minutes of treatment.

For me, there is nothing I can do to ask him not to scream so loud. Normally, if I managed to communicate with the patient, I might plead him to quiet down or at least not to scream so loud as there is really a chance that the landlord might decide not to renew my lease (though I have been there for 20 years) as it really caused so much disturbance to my neighbors. Just imagine 20 minutes of non-stop screaming.

Oh, I forgot to mention, this is a 10 sessions for 10 consecutive days' treatment course. So my nightmare has just started... 9 more sessions to go.

But then, a miracle happened on the 5th day. The boy just walked in by himself looking very proud with big bold strides, and refused to let the father carry him. He climbed up onto the treatment bed, lie down with the head on the pillow as if he is going to wait for something enjoyable.

So, I just started the treatment with no hesitation. As you might remember, it is a treatment stroking the forehead with the 2 probe electrodes. I can see Adam opened his eyes wide and followed the movement of the 2 probe electrodes. How I hope I have videotaped this funny phenomenon.

So as Adam looked so enjoyable and so fascinated by the treatment, Harry just stood by the side without climbing up to the bed to hold his son down.

While Adam kept busy tracking the movement of the probes, he suddenly stopped and sits up as he heard mommy Ada entered the clinic into the treatment room.

This is another unforgettable moment that replayed in my mind every time I mentioned this story.

ADAM OPENED HIS ARMS TO EMBRACE MOM AND KISSED HER ON THE LIPS.

Ada was overjoyed with tears running down her face and said to Adam, "You kiss auntie Milly as well!", as if she wanted me to share her happiness.

Then I thought to myself, *'Oh, no need'*. I am not used to wet kisses by strangers. Of course, I did not say this out to discourage this amazing moment but I thought I must have sent out this message in the air.

And surprisingly, Adam looked directly into my eyes and get my message. He gave me a hug on the side of my face.

At this point, I know Adam is not an autistic kid anymore!

Change the Life

To speak the truth, I am very happy with this achievement.

Because I know I really have changed the life of this boy.

Adam continued the rest of the 5 sessions and kept showing improvement. He started to have eye contact when having a conversation. He started to speak up, started to show happiness, to smile and open up himself.

Frankly, I think I changed the life of the parent as well. 5 years later, I met Ada in the street. She looked so much younger and happier instead of the look of a worried mom.

I remember I asked her permission to do a report on the newspaper of a case study on Autism right after the exciting kissing event. She was so frightened and upset and hid herself under the table begging me not to do it even though I told her it is simply a written report with false names and no photograph.

Of course, I respect her concern as parents are very sensitive to peer group stigma issue.

I hope with this book, it would be able to send out a message that there is an alternative treatment which is non-invasive without any side effect and no downtime which can change the lives of more Autistic kids and their families.

—End—

Just to let you know...

All the names mentioned in this book are not real names.

If you have any questions about this special therapy, please do not hesitate to write to

ngmilly@gmail.com

Milly would try her best to help you fi nd a solution.

Related website

www.bodyrejuvenationsystem.com

This is a series of *'How to'* books about Milly's 20 years of work as a Microcurrent Specialist in Hong Kong. Many of them are very funny and interesting that you would not want to miss!

Acknowledgements

I always felt deeply indebted to all my clients and patients who trusted me and gave me inspirations and feedback throughout my 25 years of my career life as a Microcurrent Rejuvenation Specialist. They always worried that the day I stopped working as a Physiotherapist, this special treatment would vanish with me. Please don't worry as I am going to teach through the Internet, set up online courses, video training, write books, etc. I hope this would become a global sensation. This is just the beginning. Please support me by sending a review on Amazon and social media.

My special thanks goes to Dr. Thomas Wing- the inventor of Microcurrent device. Dr. Wing was my mentor who gave me a lot of guidance and encouragement in my early practice years since 1992. Very sadly, Dr. Wing passed away in 2013 at the age of 94.

The second very important person in my early practice career who gave me the inspiration to my work today was a young 25 years old banker back in 1994. He told me the needle feeling that I accidentally generated on him made his injured knee felt a lot better, almost an instantaneous recovery. I also bet it was because of him that I earned the 19 years contract to serve the staff of HSBC until 2013 when the bank decided to cancel this benefit.

One person who is so important to my later work and boosts my confidence tremendously is Mr. Leung, empower me to design treatment on different arenas e.g. Hair regrowth, reverse hearing loss and treat tinnitus and correct joint deformities. This gentleman sustained a badly crushed hand injury trapping his hand in the electric saw with two fingers detached. It was his strong determination to recover, the high pain tolerance that brought along this incredible 100% full recovery. (Please refer to image B on page 18) After seeing this result, I started to believe that our human body has high potential to recuperate, only if you allowed this to happen. Thereafter, I started to develop a lot of different techniques, knowing that even with fractured bones, crushed cartilage, complete severed nerves, blood vessels, tendons, ligaments, our body can still recover as if nothing has happened, only if you have the willpower. I started to develop skills such as Non-Surgical Correction of Bunions/ hammer toes, permanent correction of Scoliosis without surgical intervention, Regeneration of cartilage for hips and knees saving patient from joint replacement surgery.

Best Regards,

Milly Ng, 2022

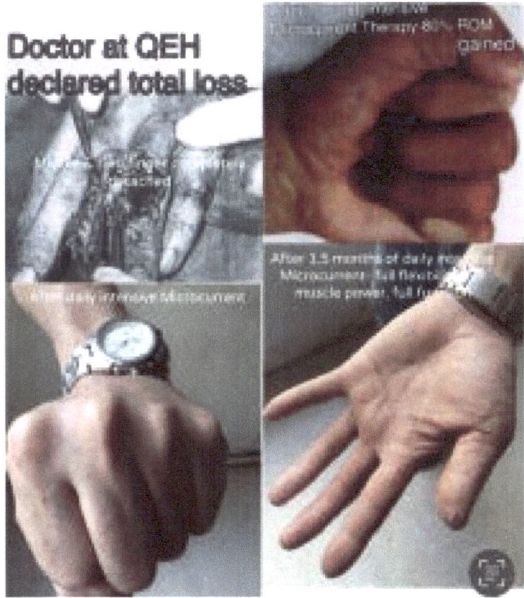

Image B

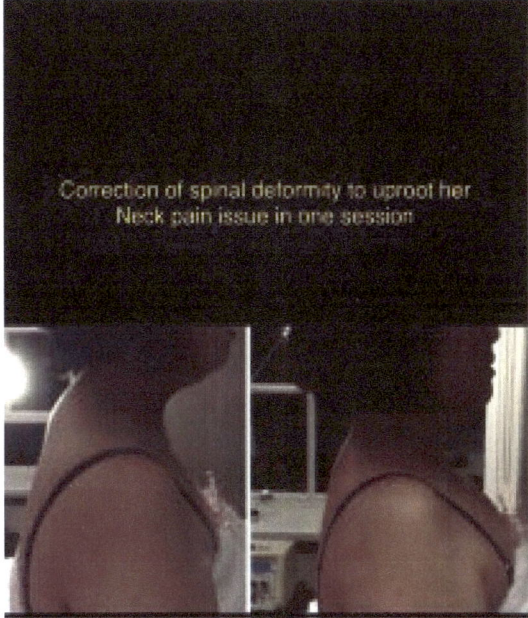

Image C

Hair regrowth for patient with
balding issue in 9 days

Before   After

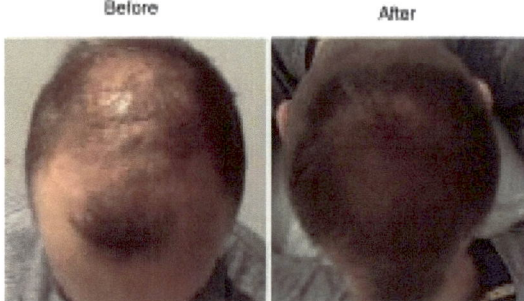

Image D

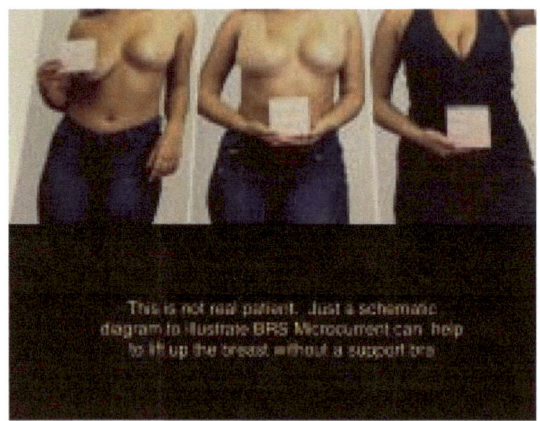

This is not real patient. Just a schematic
diagram to illustrate BRS Microcurrent can help
to lift up the breast without a support bra

Image E

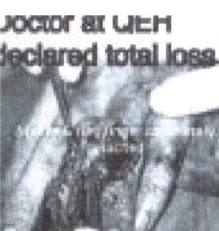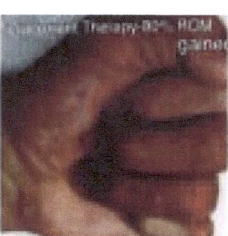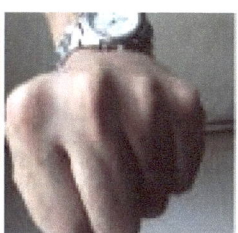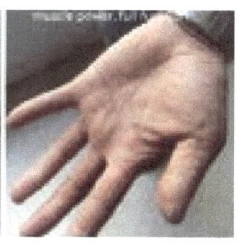

Image G

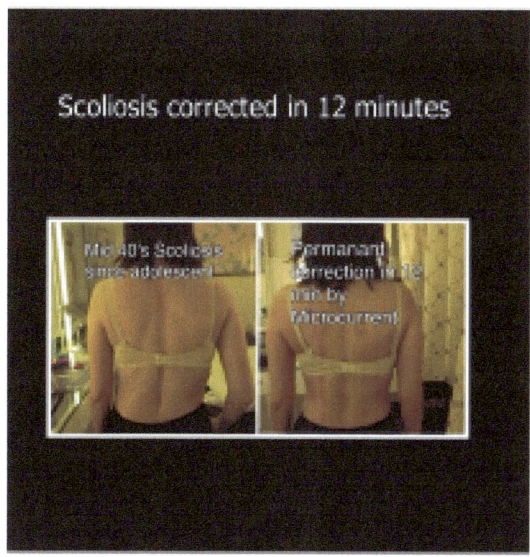

Image H

3rd degree scald healed in 15 days of
BRS Microcurrent saving patient from
skin graft

Image I

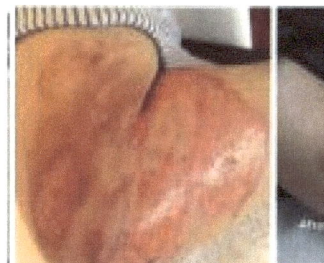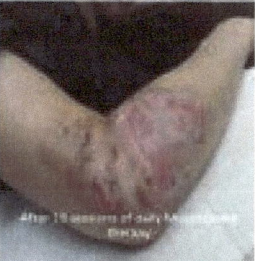

Image I

A special letter to you

So glad you have the pleasure of reading this book sharing the fun of how little Adam in just 5 days having this special treatment managed to come out of the Autism that has been bothering him and his family for more than 3 years.

I hope with this book can draw the attention of the community that Autism is not a condition that is so far-fetched. There is alternative therapy, purely natural, without any side effect and is non-invasive that is certainly worth to try and explore.

Milly has treated quite a number of Autistic kids at different stages and different age.

She once treated a 15 years old boy with high function autism. At home he seldom talked to his mom but in my clinic during the treatment, he would talk non stopped. It was also very funny that when I stopped whirling the 2 probes on his forehead, he would stop immediately, and start talking again once I resume the whirling. Like as if turning off and turning on a recording. I still remember on one occasion, I am going to visit Tampa, Florida in my next holiday. So I told him and then this 15 years old kid in this 20 min of treatment starting telling me everything, every details about Tampa, the weather in different climate, the population, the economy, the famous attractions, as if he was reciting from the encyclopedia. It was amazing!

Another interesting case was a 9 years old girl who came

from San Francisco to visit Hong Kong for holiday with Kawasaki disease having symptoms presentation similar to Autism. After treated her for 1 session, Milly asked the family how was it going. They told her that grandfather was most impressed. The reason is this 9 years old girl before the treatment when eating out with the family, she would eat with her hands. Just imagine in a 5-star hotel restaurant where everyone dressed up for the occasion, it is very odd to see a girl picking up the food from the plate with her hands. But then just after the first treatment, somehow this young lady started to eat with fork and knife for the first time in her life. Somehow she just picked up the cue of what everybody is doing. Somehow the BRS Microcurrent treatment has turn on the switch for her.

Like Autism, there are many diseases and conditions that traditional medicine has not find a cure or that there simply take a pill or a surgical removal to replace with a prosthetic part is not the answer. I would highly suggest why don't we explore this arena of self-rejuvenation by introducing this Microcurrent to target the problem cells to recover. All you need is to try, no downside and there is no issue of addiction, no worry of side effects as it is simply our own body current. If it works, good! If it doesn't work, no harm done!

In order to promote this special procedure, I need a lot of these BRS Microcurrent. So, I started to explore to find a manufacture facility that can help to produce this Special medical device to make sure people who would like to learn using it can have the instrument to operate on. Since 2012 when the original manufacturer in Los Angeles stopped the production line, despite many to and fro discussion in emails and few personal visits over the years. Up to a point they promised the production but I have to sign an agreement that I would not sell the device in US. All these because of the scrutiny of FDA. With no other option at that moment, I have to agree on the proposal, but in the last minute, they still refused to continue the production. Thereafter, I searched all over the world, from many other facilities in US, UK and China. Actually I have approached one of the biggest medical device manufacturer in US to discuss the production. They produced a small unit for home use and a combo unit for professional use. During the discussion, I voiced out I would like to test its efficacy. So the owner takes out their prototype to have a test run. Then I said as it should be able to show immediate results, do you guys have any area that is painful or have issue that needs treatment? The owner of the facility somehow had a big scar on his palm, so I worked on the scar for him. But then it didn't show anything with the combo unit. So I brought out my own device from my car and worked on him, it gave him sharp needle feeling during the few seconds of treatment and an immediate loosening feeling of his scar. Then I know his combo device is not the one I am looking for.

Luckily in 2018, one of my girl friend's husband introduced his partner who is in this medical device electronic production to help me. And voila, we have our own production and on Nov 29, 2021, we obtained the FDA registration, which meant we can officially market and sell the device in US and global.

In 2021, Milly Ng has relocated her practice from Hong Kong to Arcadia, Los Angeles.

HUNTINGTON BODY REJUVENATION CENTRE

289 W HUNTINGTON DR
SUITE 204
ARCADIA. CA 91007
Tel: 1(626)461-5084 (Direct line) 1(562)298-8766
(WhatsApp)

It is a facility that you can come and try on the result of the device and purchase directly or if it is inconvenient to come personally, we can deliver the device to you and learn through the video step by step.

For any enquiries, please do not hesitate to call or email Milly directly, she is happy to answer your questions personally!

I hope through this message, can help ease a lot more people in all over the world to ease of their suffering and pain, to overcome their disability, to enjoy a wonderful life. Especially during the Covid pandemic, it is not convenient to visit the hospital or clinic, having a device at home to start the treatment should be a great option.

Again, thank you for your patron and may you keep healthy and have happiness and joy!

Sincerely, Milly Ng

Huntington Body Rejuvenation
Centre CA, USA Feb 2022

www.ingramcontent.com/pod-product-compliance
Lightning Source LLC
Chambersburg PA
CBHW040900120626
46551CB00001B/106